T0193505

Jennifer has always had to hurry to grow up. At eight years old, her father abandoned her, leaving her in the care of others. At twenty three years old, she asked him why he never came back for her. He replied, because she never apologized to him for burdening him with her birth. To process the ugly truth, her first step was to start a journal...

NAME:
BIRTHDAY:
FAVORITE COLOR:
STRENGTH:
WEAKNESS:

In case of lost, please return this book to this address:

_____

_____

In Search of My
HEART

Coloring Journal

JENNIFER VERDIEU

authorHOUSE®

If this is correct then the equation is also the solution,
but developing the theorem is the actual problem.
X,y,z are They really unknown?

AuthorHouse™
1663 Liberty Drive
Bloomington, IN 47403
www.authorhouse.com
Phone: 1 (800) 839-8640

Published by AuthorHouse 10/03/2018

ISBN: 978-1-5462-4804-0 (sc)
ISBN: 978-1-5462-4803-3 (hc)
ISBN: 978-1-5462-4802-6 (e)

Library of Congress Control Number: 2018907260

Print information available on the last page.

TO PEN.

CHAPTER 1

ANTE PERICARDIUM

TITLE

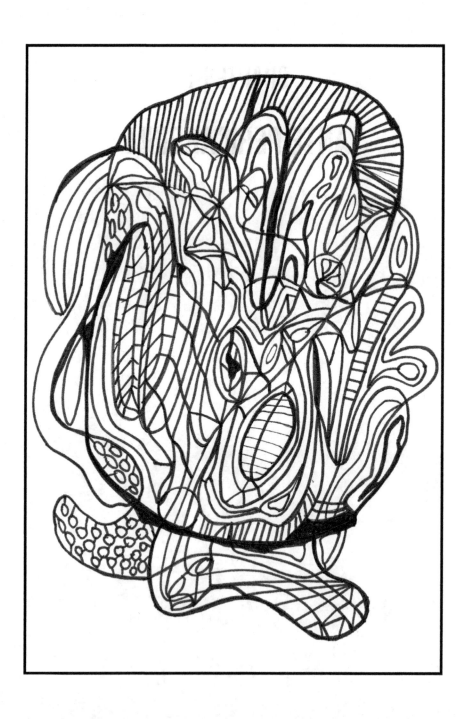

TITLE

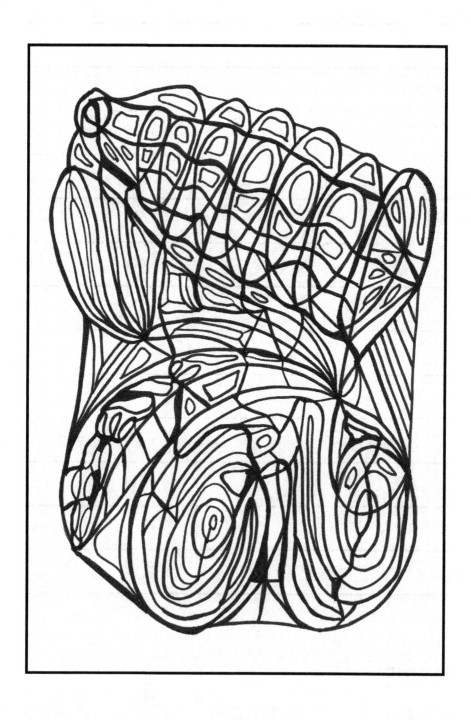

DATE

TIME

TITLE

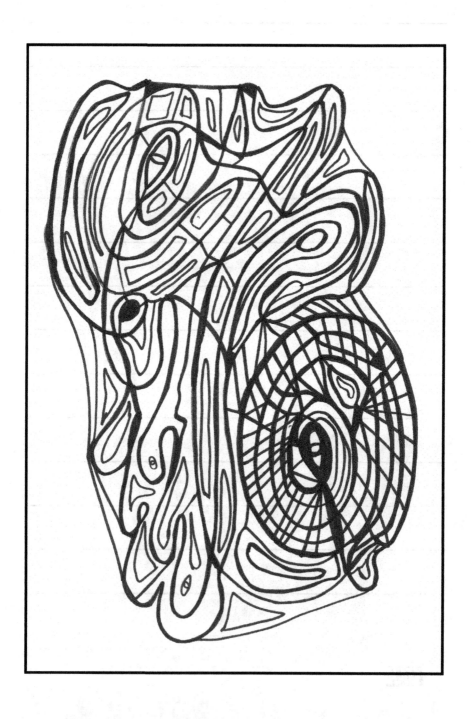

TITLE

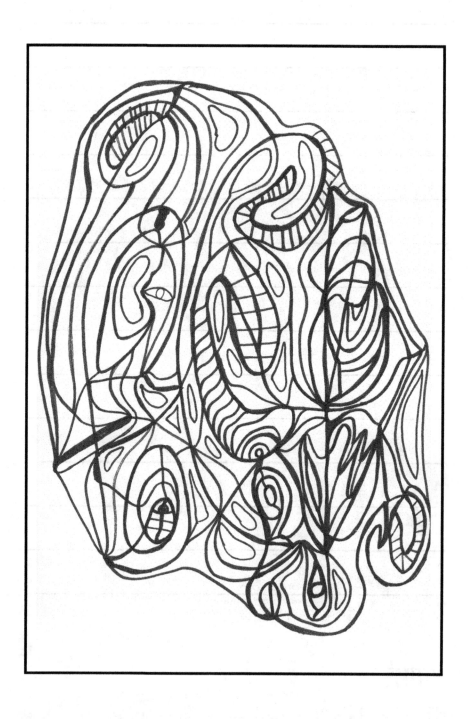

_____

_____

_____

_____

_____

_____

_____

_____

_____

_____

_____

_____

TITLE

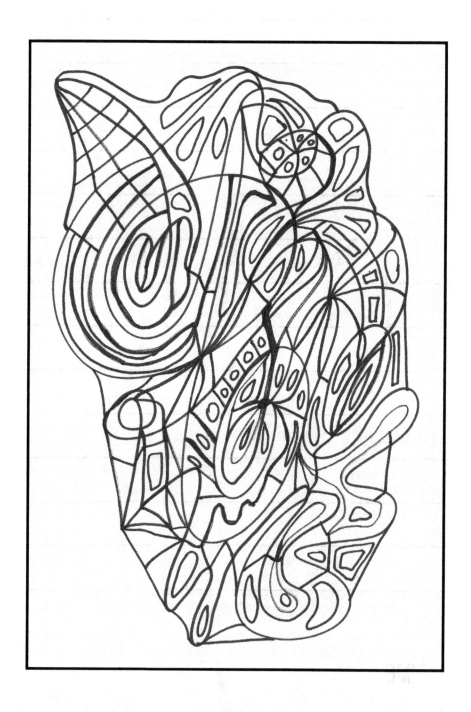

DATE

TIME

TITLE

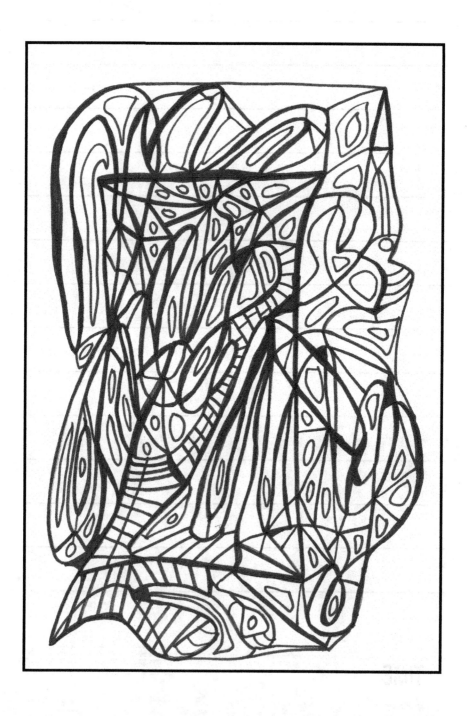

DATE

TIME

TITLE

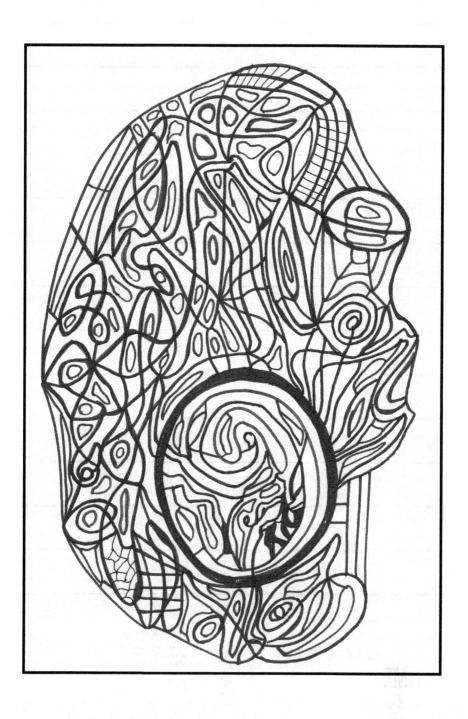

TITLE

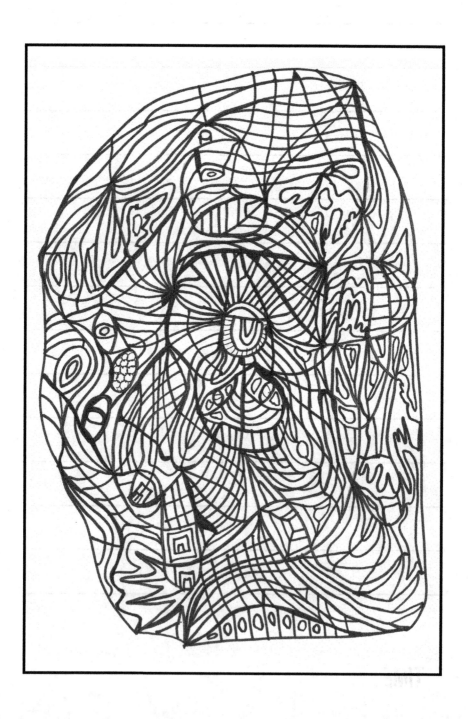

DATE

TIME

TITLE

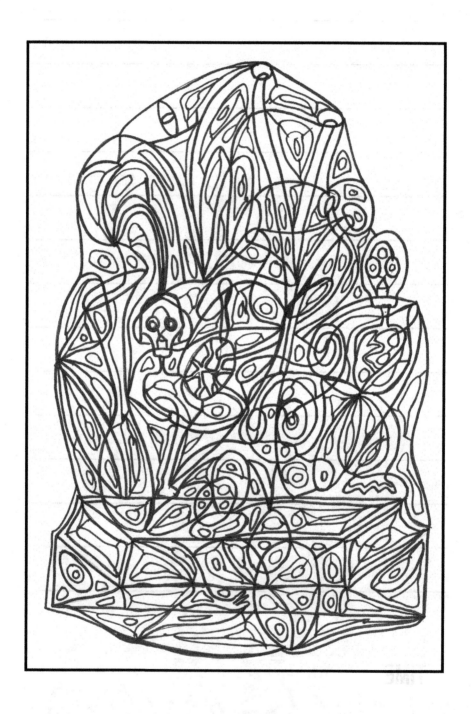

TITLE

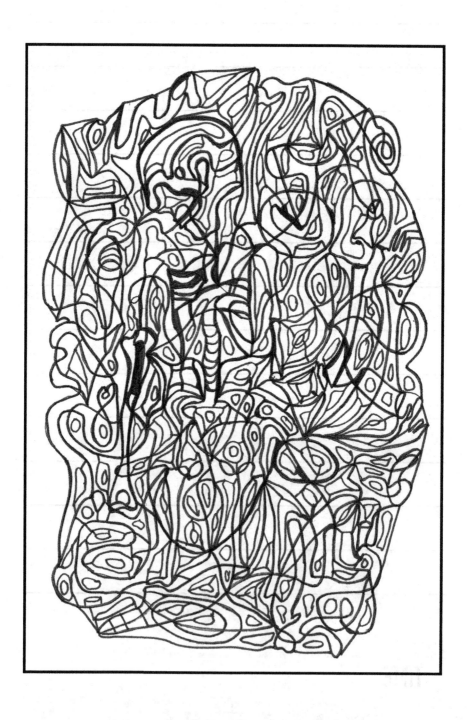

_____

_____

_____

_____

_____

_____

_____

_____

_____

_____

_____

CHAPTER 2

INTRA IN VENTRICULUM

TITLE

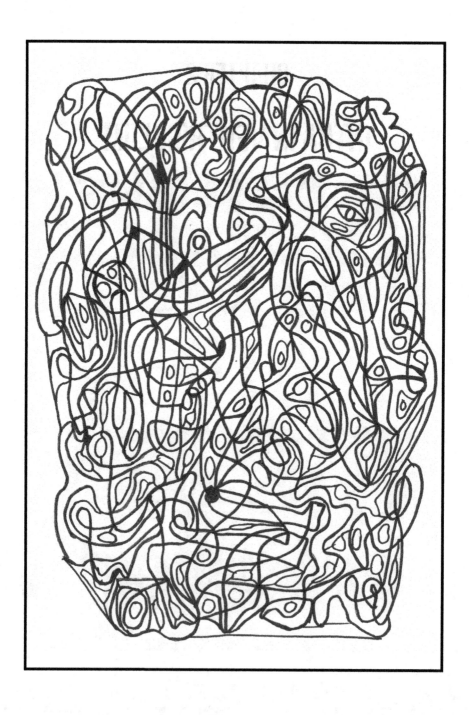

DATE

TIME

TITLE

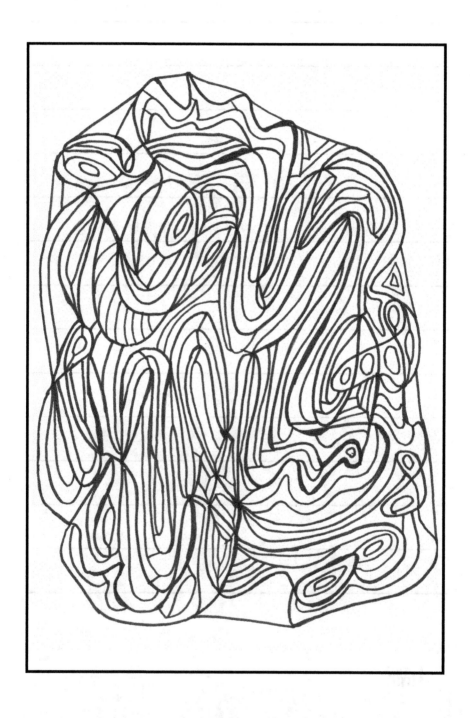

DATE

TIME

TITLE

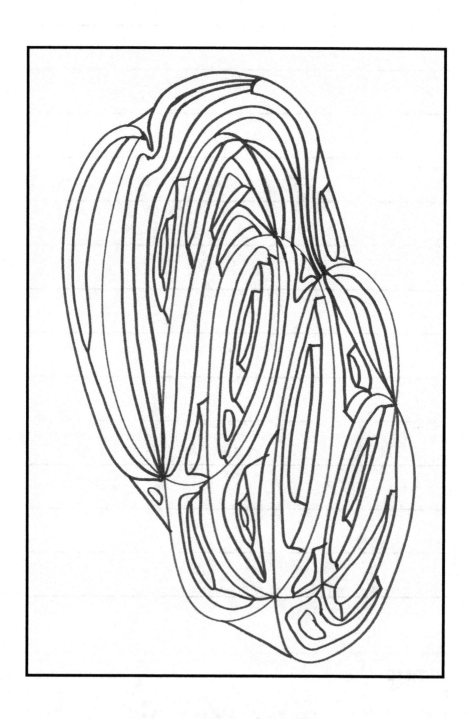

TITLE

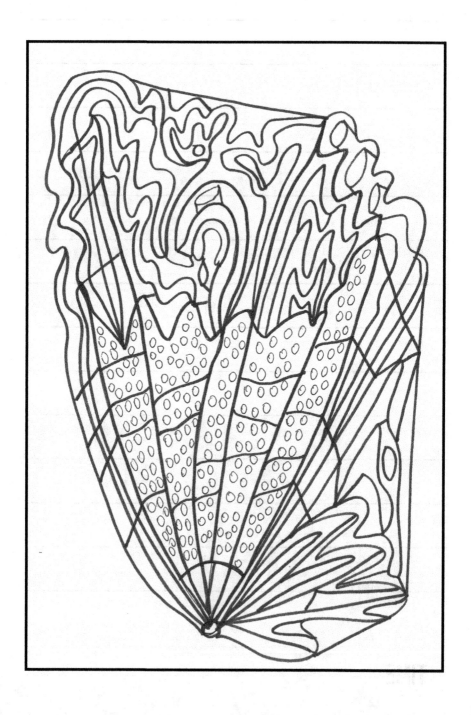

TITLE

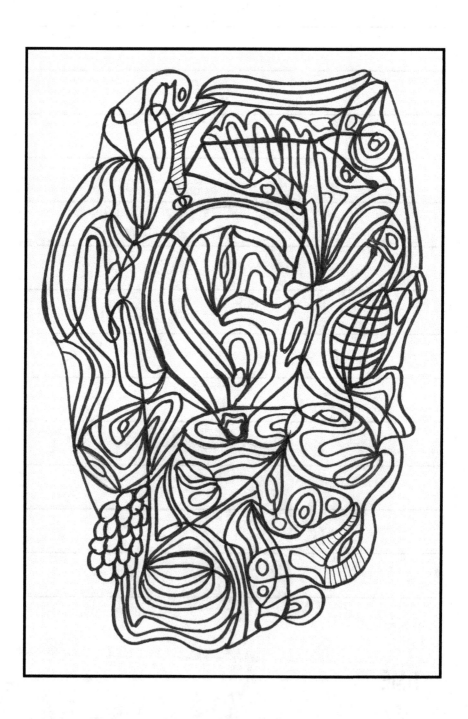

DATE

TIME

TITLE

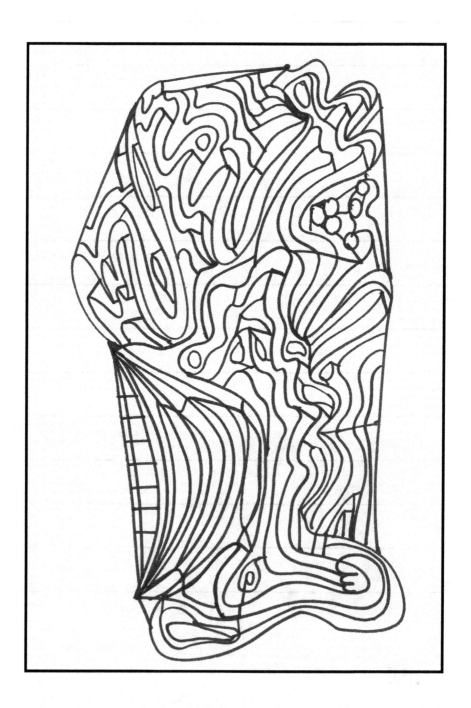

TITLE

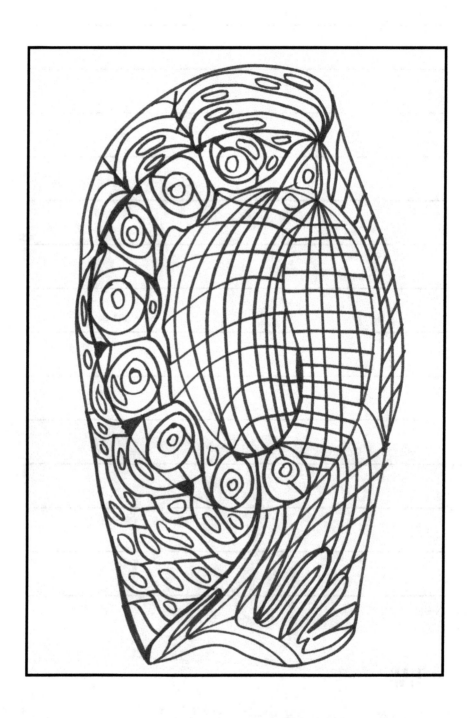

TITLE

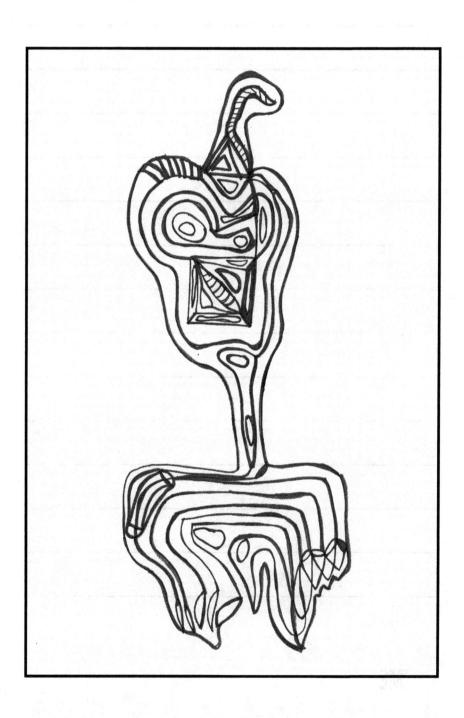

TITLE

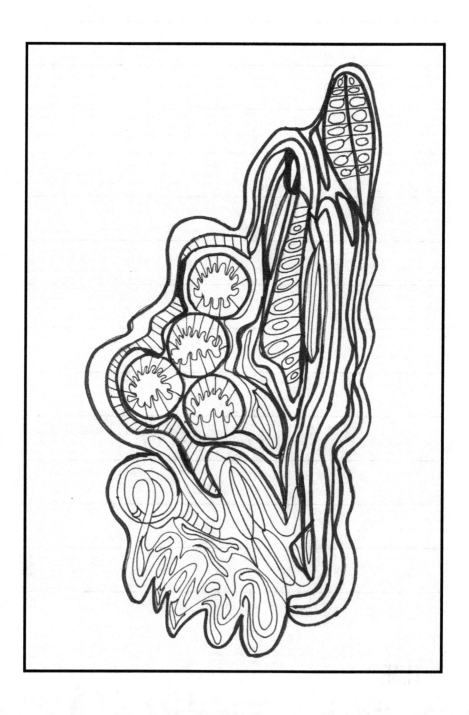

DATE

TIME

TITLE

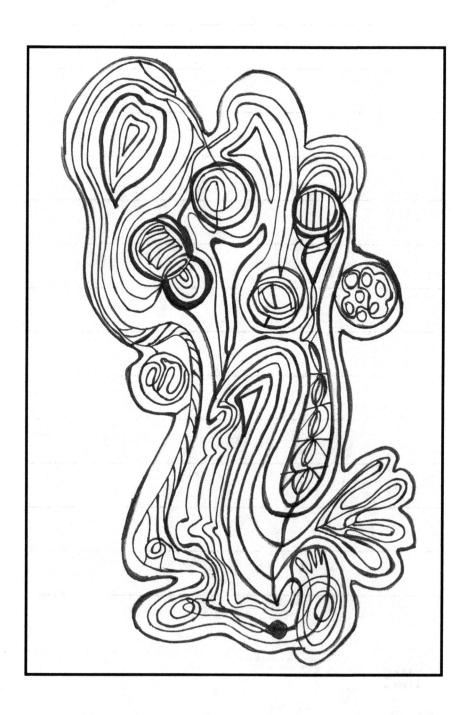

_____

_____

_____

_____

_____

_____

_____

_____

_____

_____

_____

_____

CHAPTER 3

ACCELERATIO

TITLE

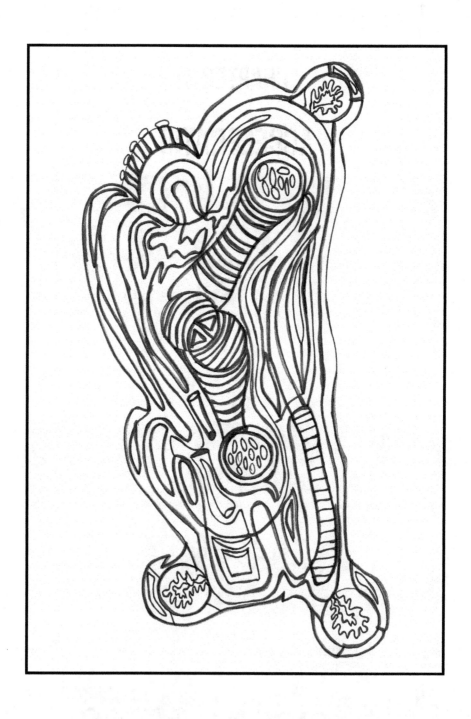

TITLE

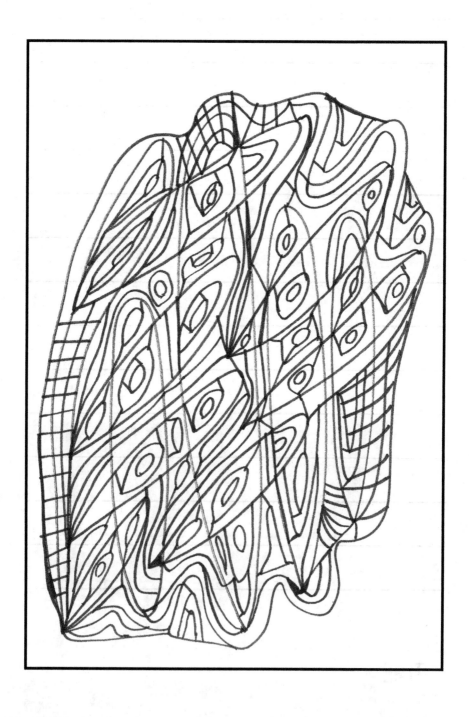

TITLE

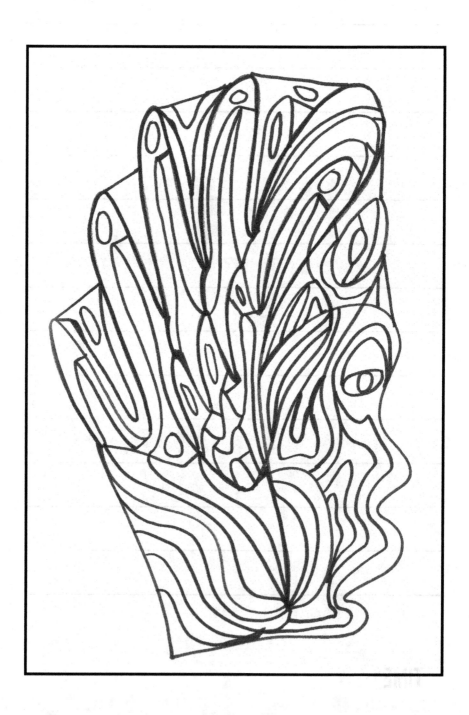

DATE

TIME

TITLE

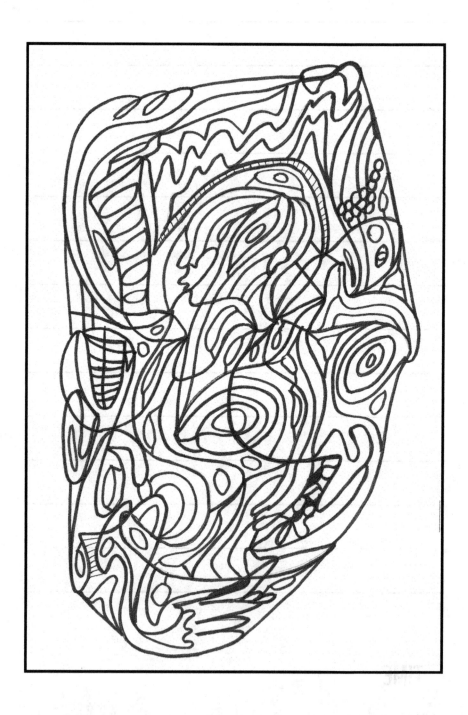

TITLE

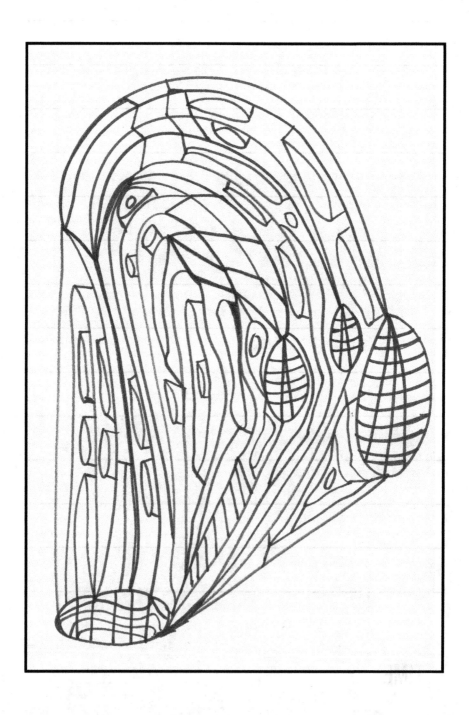

TITLE

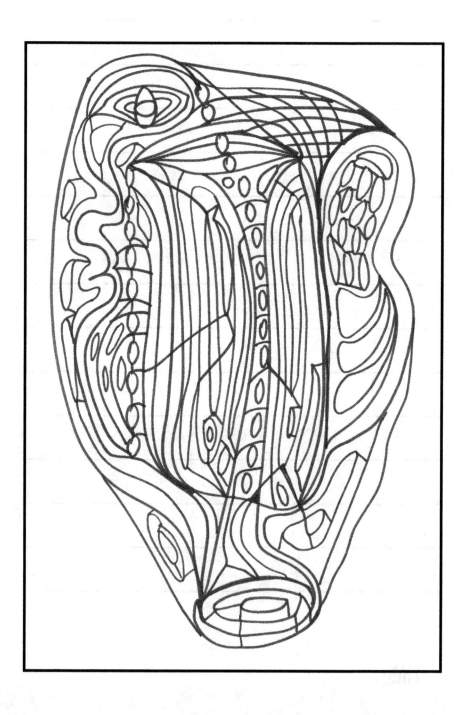

TITLE

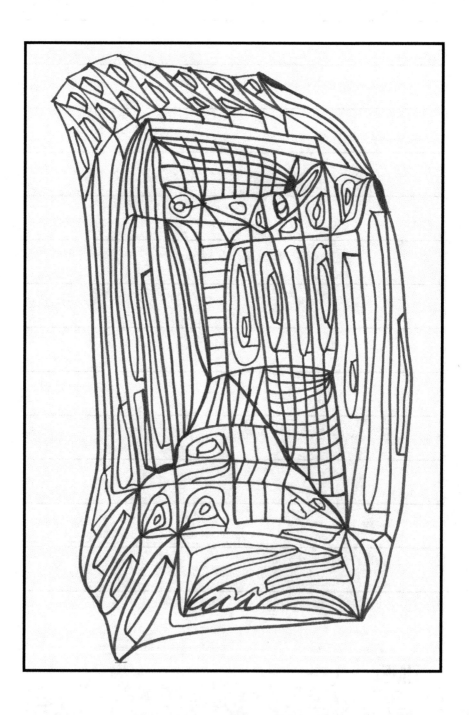

TITLE

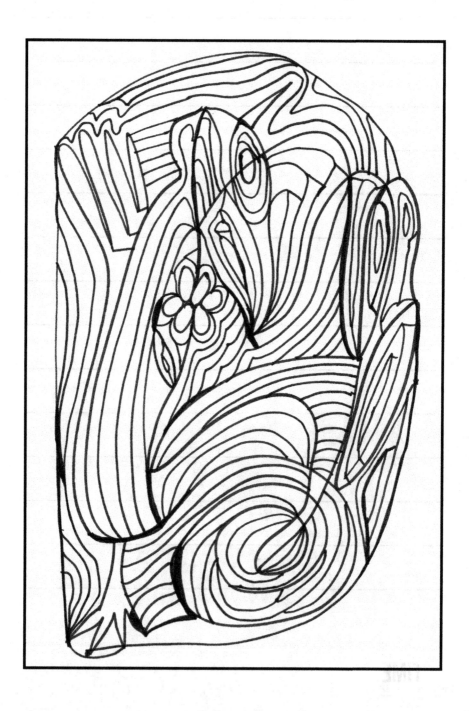

TITLE

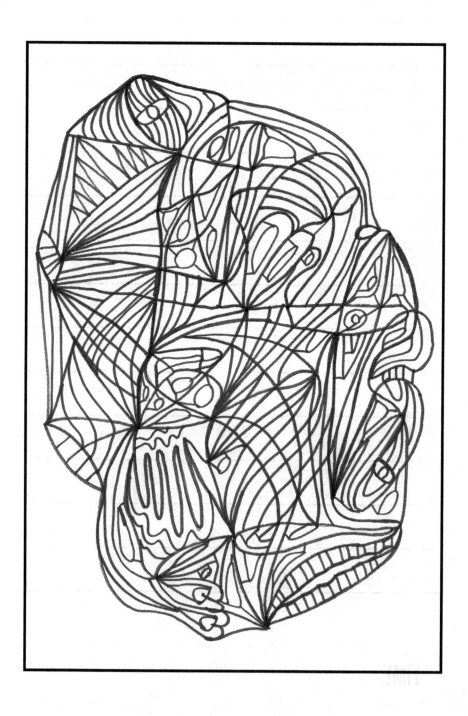

TITLE

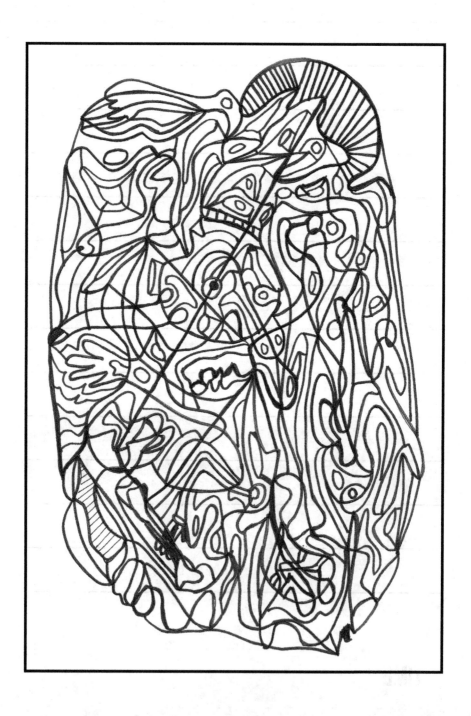

_____

_____

_____

_____

_____

_____

_____

_____

_____

_____

_____

_____

CHAPTER 4

NIGRUM ET RIBRUM SANGUINEM

TITLE

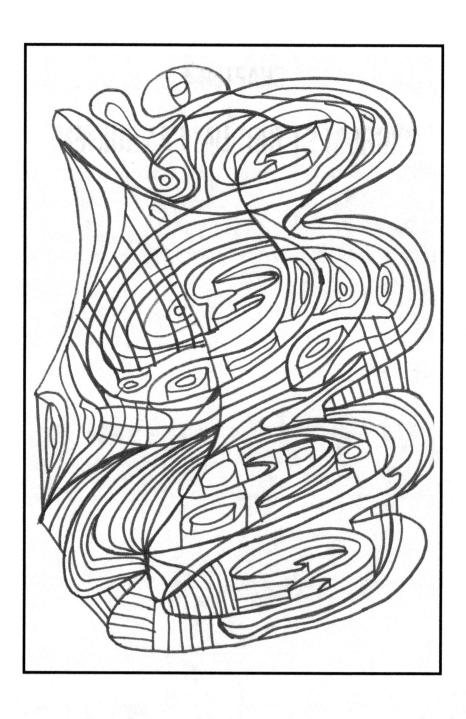

DATE

TIME

TITLE

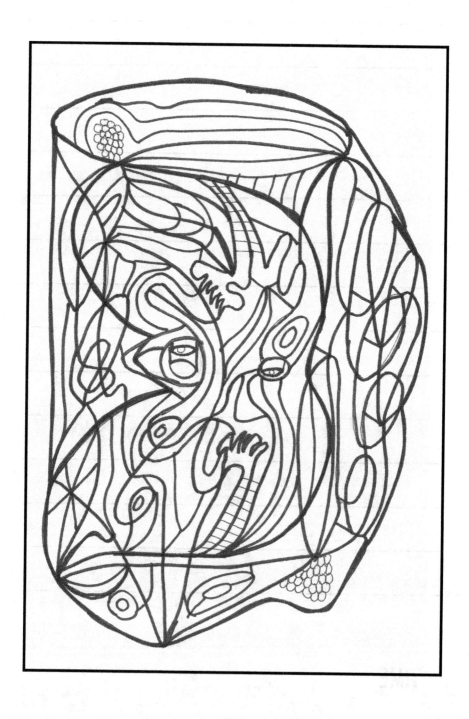

DATE

DATE

TIME

TITLE

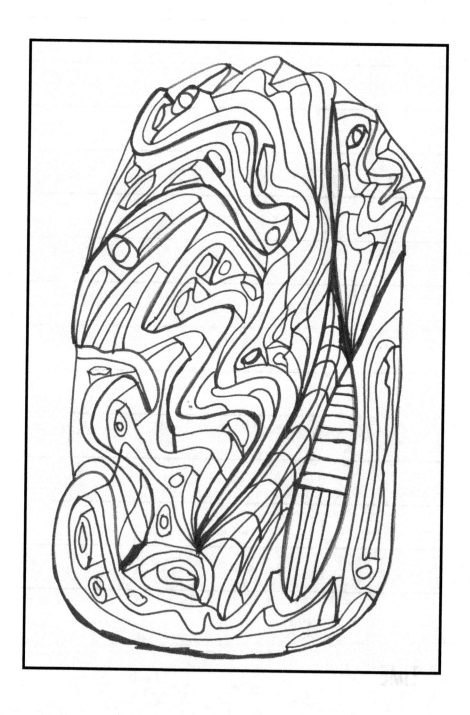

TITLE

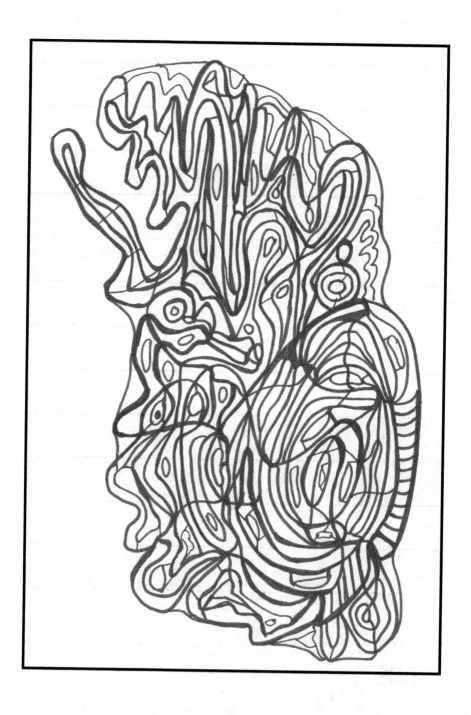

DATE

TIME

TITLE

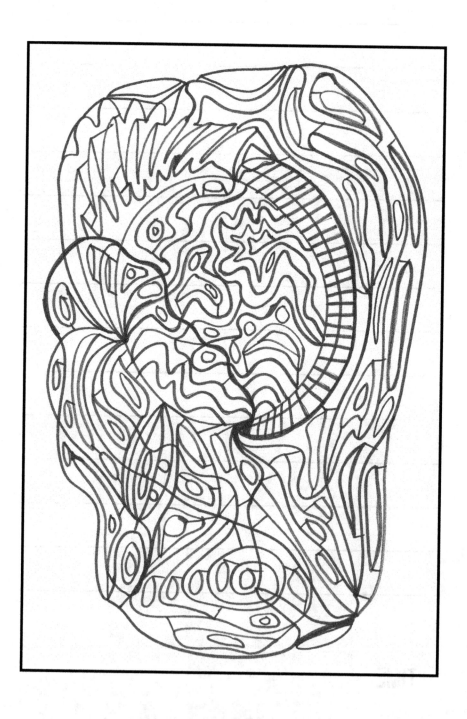

TITLE

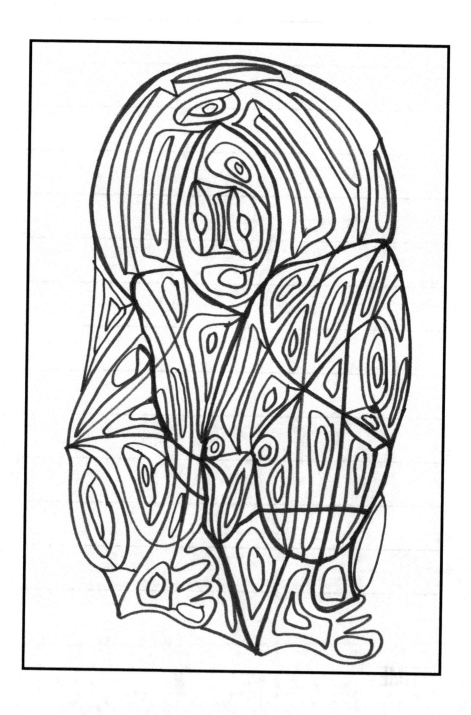

TITLE

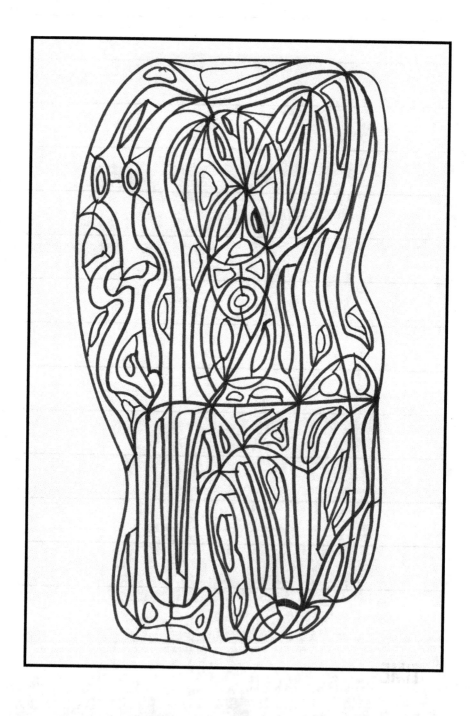

TITLE

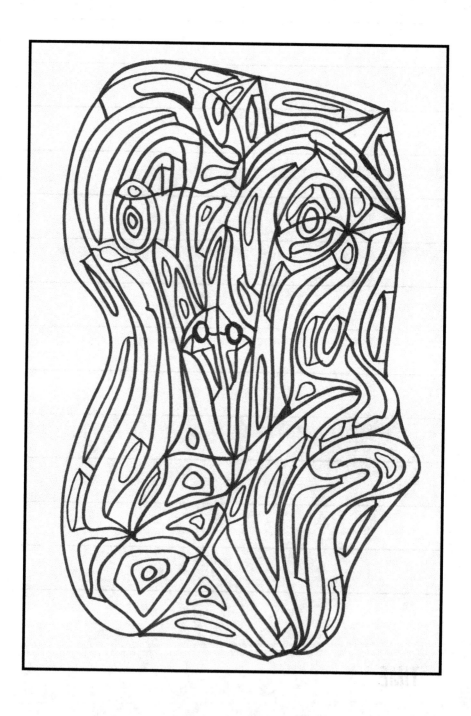

TITLE

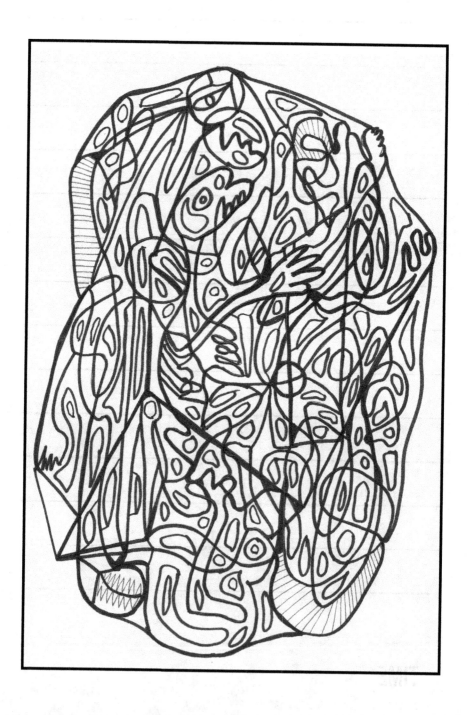

TITLE

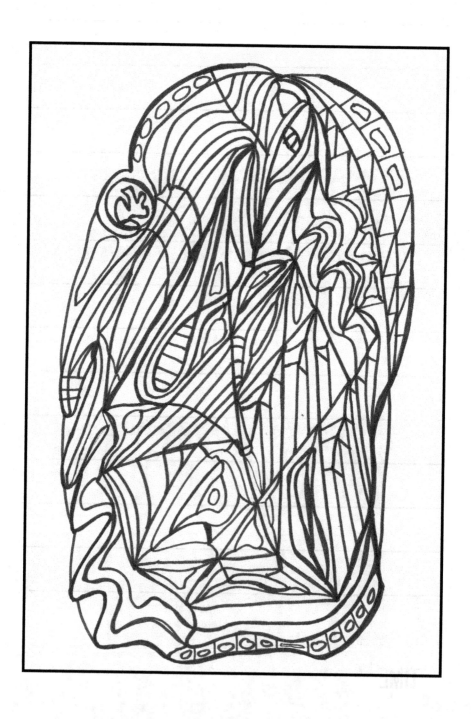

DATE

_____

_____

_____

_____

_____

_____

_____

_____

_____

_____

_____

_____

TIME

CHAPTER 5

ET VIOLOLINIST

TITLE

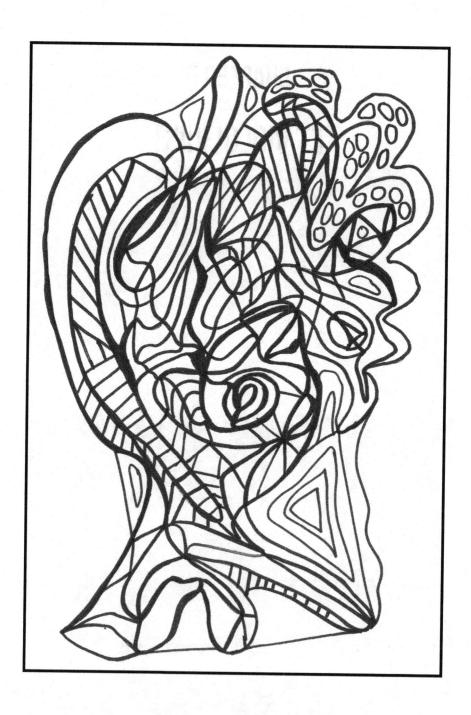

TITLE

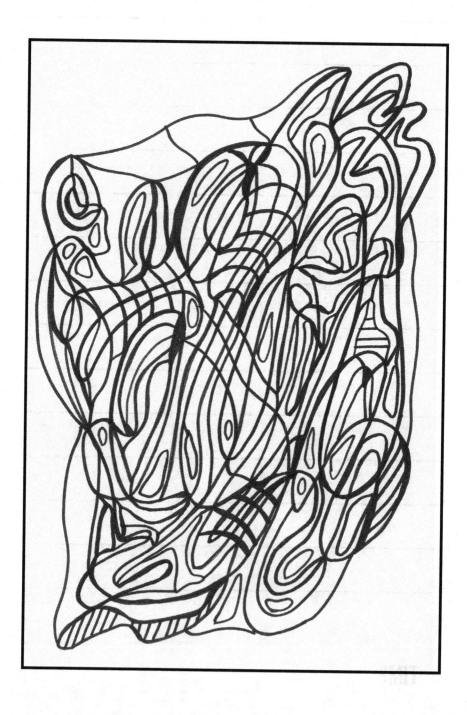

TITLE

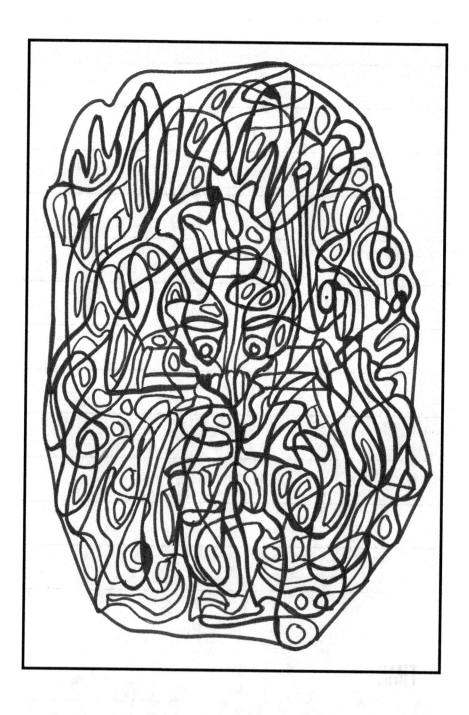

Printed in the United States
By Bookmasters